# Meet Me Where I Am

Navigating the Intersection of Autism and OCD

Elizabeth Ives Field

Autism Fieldwork

Copyright ©2023 by Elizabeth Ives Field

All rights reserved.

No portion of this book may be reproduced in any form without written permission from the publisher or author, except as permitted by U.S. copyright law.

This publication is designed to provide accurate and authoritative information in regard to the subject matter covered. It is sold with the understanding that neither the author nor the publisher is engaged in rendering legal, investment, accounting or other professional services. While the publisher and author have used their best efforts in preparing this book, they make no representations or warranties with respect to the accuracy or completeness of the contents of this book and specifically disclaim any implied warranties of merchantability or fitness for a particular purpose. No warranty may be created or extended by sales representatives or written sales materials. The advice and strategies contained herein may not be suitable for your situation. You should consult with a professional when appropriate. Neither the publisher nor the author shall be liable for any loss of profit or any other commercial damages, including but not limited to special, incidental, consequential, personal, or other damages.

Book cover design and image by Beverly Stessel

# Blurbs

<u>Meet Me Where I Am</u> is a fascinating narrative about Sam, a uniquely wired and rather brilliant autistic who works alongside his extraordinarily creative speech pathologist to uncover who Sam is and how he and the world can comingle. If you like linguistics, human sensitivity, learning theory and a positive approach to learning style differences, this book is a must read.

**Liane Holliday Willey, EdD**   Author of:

<u>Pretending to be Normal: Living with Aspergers Syndrome;</u>

<u>Safety Skills for Asperger Women: How to Save a Perfectly Good Female Life;</u>

This account of Sam's struggle to navigate a world full of blatant and hidden rules is beautifully written by Elizabeth.

We are invested in Sam from the start and her writing exudes such love and empathy for him as well as solid support and guidance as his SLP. Most importantly, we hear Sam's voice throughout and his fascinating insight into autism, OCD and extreme anxiety.

I thoroughly enjoyed it from start to finish and will be signposting it to parents and professionals on its release.

**Jacqui Rochester**, Wellbeing and Therapy Coordinator and Autism Practitioner at Mountfield Health School, University of Birmingham, Langney, England

Finished reading the book last night. Was worth reading on a few different levels. One is, that it is always interesting to read case studies and see how other pro's handled them. Another is to learn different perspectives on how others view the student/client, etc. It reminds people that the method they use and advocate for, is not always the best... Another thing I thought about was how different diagnosis, in this case, autism and ocd, are seldom enough information to know where to begin or how to proceed. Sam certainly presented with symptoms of autism and ocd, but that info doesn't really matter. What matters is who he is and what works with him. Your title was a good choice ...I really enjoyed reading the book.

**Ben Wolfson**, autism specialist, author of Tasso the Turtle

...no comments just accolades. A wonderful and important story.

**Susan B. Woods**, Professional Development consultant. www.susanbwoods.com

Your book reads well and easy - you wrote with an open heart that drew me in to the story of how Sam grew and developed into a young man. I liked the positive nature of the story, how Sam contributed, and of course how it all has ended up so far. Thanks for letting me read it.

**Judy Benz Duncan**, Occupational Therapist, Mentor, Consultant, Published Author

For Samuel Stessel and his parents, Robert and Beverly Stessel, with many thanks for sharing their lives and helping me to share our story with others.

# Contents

Introduction — IX

1. Speech and the Postmaster — 1
2. The Postmaster Lingers On — 11
3. And Wait, There's More — 21
4. Samuel Says — 31
5. In and Out of School — 39
6. Life Happens — 49
7. Excursions and Discussions — 63
8. The Year Between Schools — 81
9. A Glance Back — 93
10. High School and Beyond — 101
11. Now and Later — 113

| Acknowledgments | 121 |
| About Author | 123 |

# Introduction

At age ten, Samuel's considerable intellectual gifts were complicated by autism, obsessive compulsive disorder and the extreme anxiety that accompanies both of these disabilities. As a result, Sam had developed several unique communication differences, unwavering avoidance of any hint that adults were controlling him, and other challenging behaviors that disrupted harmony at home, school and in the community.

This is a book about the "I" in IEP. Special education teams create Individual Education Plans for their students that include accommodations and goals for the next year. Some students require minor, moderate, or significant supports and modifications of the curriculum, but others, like Samuel, can only survive in public school with a highly individualized program.

This non-fiction story tells of Samuel's adventures in academic, social, and practical education over the course of a dozen years. In addition to the common autism struggles with personal interactions, eating, sleeping and hygiene disturbances, changes and unpredictability, Sam was contending with an invisible postmaster who stole many of his words, panic in response to asymmetrical touch, an unyielding inability to comply with adult directives, and a myriad of other issues.

Told from the perspective of speech/language pathologist and autism consultant Elizabeth Field, with input from the now-adult Sam and his supportive parents, the book was written from a seven-inch high stack of notes and reports and from fond memories. All of it was carefully proofread and fact-checked by Samuel, who also contributed anecdotes and strong opinions in several chapters.

The book is entirely true, as creative nonfiction must be, and it weaves the story of our neurodivergent and neurotypical collaboration with the themes of highly individualized education, the consequences of anxiety, and the benefits of acceptance, trust, innovation, patience, and humor.

My first book, <u>Building Communication and Independence for Children Across the Autism Spectrum,</u> addressed issues of communication and interactive behavior that occur frequently among children throughout the autism spectrum. The goals and interventions described apply to many children and are rooted in practices based on research and on my repeated clinical experiences.

But this book is about unique or unusual challenges connected to autism that I have encountered only once or a few times in my career. If you are a parent of one or more children with autism or a teacher or therapist for many, you will encounter some but perhaps not all, of the challenges described in this book. If you are an autistic adult, you may have significant opinions about the educational journey and about our approach to it. I hope my writing illustrates that the process of building relationships and intervening therapeutically is an art as well as a science and often involves individualized creativity along with evidence-based practices. Sometimes this requires accepting that another person's reality may be very different from your own.

# Chapter 1

# Speech and the Postmaster

Peering up at me from behind round glasses framed by shoulder-length brown hair, Samuel announced, "The postmaster stole my words and hid them in the dead letter office."

"Ahhh," I replied, trying to decide what to say next.

Ten-year-old Samuel had a diagnosis on the autism spectrum and his school team had asked me to make recommendations about his highly unusual but very consistent speech patterns. After years of home schooling, Sam began attending public school in fourth grade. Since then, he had been increasingly reinventing common words in ways unique to him. Once he changed them, the words stayed changed. He never accidentally said them correctly.

As a result, he was becoming less and less intelligible and his mother, Beverly, often had to interpret for him. Among his unique speech substitutions were:

*es* for *yes*

*yee* for *you*

*woo-erd* for *word*

*haggy* for *hungry*

*mead* for *me*

*one-pour* for *fourteen* and a substitution of *p* for *f* in most other words

And Sam had eliminated the words *What, Who, Where*, and *Why*. If he needed one of these, he simply replaced it with *When*.

Although Samuel used these and other changes consistently in his own speech, he did say the conventional words when speaking through his stuffed toys, a sock monkey named Bim (short for "Born-in-Maine,") and the cartoon tiger

Hobbes, created by his very artistic mother. After protesting to Beverly, "When (*why*) are yee making mead do this?" Sam demonstrated that he could indeed say *yes, hungry,* and other words from the list if he was speaking as Bim or Hobbes. Apparently, the postmaster had taken the correct versions of the words only from Sam, not from Bim and Hobbes.

Beverly explained, "We understand him at home. I think he talks that way so I will have to be there to translate for him." That sounded right to me.

Also, a whole category of words had gone missing. Samuel proclaimed that his polite words and greetings were in separate packages deep in the back of the dead letter office. Apparently, when he was six years old, the adults at Samuel's private school had insisted that he should, "say the magic words," so these words had run away and later been captured by the postmaster. Now, four years later, he still could not utter *please, thank you, hello, goodbye* or similar polite or greeting words, ever.

Since my mission was to recommend ways to improve this situation, I thought it prudent to ask what had already been tried. Samuel's speech/language pathologist had described her attempts at prompting, discussion, role playing, using social stories, and studying how polite words were used in different cultures. His parents had given him a basket of small papers with words like *please, thank you* and *excuse me* which he could, but rarely did, hand to people instead of saying the polite words. And, as suggested by his parents, Sam would, on rare occasions, use alternatives like "I appreciate that you …" because he could not say "Thank you." Unfortunately, neither these paper words nor the alternative phrases were accepted substitutes for polite words at school.

Because Sam was again learning at home, we met there. He and his mother guided me on a thorough and detailed excursion through their home and yard. The school team had described Sam as generally uncommunicative except to get his needs met, but he participated eagerly in this tour, verbally and physically taking the lead whenever possible. Unlike her son, Beverly is reliably talkative, and she had become accustomed to explaining Samuel to others, so he sometimes needed to interrupt. He did so persistently.

As we walked, I learned, through Sam's somewhat fragmented and disjointed expository speech and his mother's clarifications, that Sam's trusted paraprofessional had left the school, the school was repeatedly calling Beverly to take him home because of some disruptive behavior or other, and he was complaining of frequent stomach upsets and headaches. So, his parents chose to resume homeschooling and work toward some resolution for the next year.

We ended our tour with a visit to a wonderful miniature village Samuel and Beverly had created in his bedroom. The town was known as Stesselville and included a seven-story school, complete with behavioral rules which Sam had read in his mother's psychology texts and posted on the walls of the miniature building. The Stesselville postmaster's dead letter office, containing the missing words, was in Sam's closet.

So here we were, back at the discussion of the postmaster's word theft. My best response at that juncture seemed to be "Why?"

"Because he is grouchy," Samuel replied.

"Do you think we could get him to give them back?" I asked. "You deserve to have your words."

"Maybe, if he was in a good mood."

This led to some pondering of how we might improve this invisible postmaster's mood. Perhaps we could give him something? We settled on the idea of trading the damaged words for their conventional counterparts, so Samuel made the first of several trips upstairs to check on the postmaster's mood. Not good at the moment.

Next, we decided on the order in which he would request the return of his words, grouping them into packages according to the first letter in the words. After consulting a dictionary and finding that there were only three problem words beginning with *Y*, we had our first target. He made it clear that the polite words would not be recoverable this way, as they were buried too deep in the dead letter office. I did not argue. Another check of the closet determined that the postmaster was still grumpy.

We decided Sam could package the *Y* words to trade later when the postmaster's mood improved. Samuel had stopped writing anything by hand, evidently in resistance to a determined occupational therapist who had insistently corrected his formation of letters, so he thumped off to the computer to make package labels for the defective words. His thumping gait was the result of Sam refusing for several years to allow his left heel to touch the floor. But that's another story.

# MEET ME WHERE I AM

As I was getting into my car to leave, and still talking with Beverly, Sam stuck his head out the door and asked how he should indicate the defective words.

"How about an asterisk?"

"Okay!" and he scurried off.

Driving home, having thoroughly enjoyed the visit, I wondered if anything would come of it.

A few days later, my phone rang. I had been told that Sam hated to talk on the phone, so I was surprised to hear his voice saying, "Is it you?" (not "yee"). When I had proven my identity to his satisfaction, he declared, "I got three woo-erds back; *yes, you* and *yesterday*. I want to get *W* back next."

The next week Beverly called to say that Sam had been ill for several days but had never wavered from using the recovered *Y* words correctly.

A couple of weeks passed, and he reported, "I got back my *W* words". They were no longer "woo-erds." A major gain from that package was the recovery of all the *Wh*-question words. Sam now didn't need to substitute *when* for *why, what, who* and *where*, making his questions much easier to understand.

He said *T* words would be next, but reminded me, without actually saying the absent expression of gratitude, that *thank you* would not be in that package "because polite words are packaged separately in the dead letter office; locked up, and the key is lost."

Two months after my initial consultation at his home, I found a phone message from Sam saying I should call him. Beverly answered and I could hear Sam running to the phone saying, "Don't tell her!" He had now recovered his *T* and *F* words which he demonstrated by saying "four, five, fourteen", and "I want my father to fix it. Next, I'll get my *J* words."

This process went on over the course of nine months while his mother, father and I did nothing but admire his progress. We had a celebratory lobster casserole dinner at his home when he had thirteen packages of words recovered and another when, just a week later, he had all twenty-six. I gave him a trophy with his name and accomplishment inscribed.

Rarely did Sam misuse one of the recovered words, and his speech was now error-free and easy to understand. He did provide himself with some insurance by saying that if he relapsed the error would go back to the postmaster, leaving him with the correct version. His father, Stes, confirmed later that Sam willingly repaired his occasional misuse of a recovered word if they simply reminded him that he could now say that word correctly.

And the polite words? They were still under lock and key in the dead letter office.

# Chapter 2

# The Postmaster Lingers On

The postmaster had now relinquished the common neutral words he had stolen from Sam, but he retained the vocabulary of routine social interaction. The dead letter package we called "polite words," including *please, thank you,* and *excuse me* also held greetings and farewells. So, words like *hello, bye* and *good night* were absent from Sam's speech.

I've known many children with autism who neglect or avoid these expressions, quite possibly because they are just social words and carry no obvious factual meaning. Some children are confused by them, especially by *thank you* which they may say as they give, rather than receive an object. But rarely have I seen children so adamantly vigilant about never uttering these words. Teachers and other adults had expected Sam to use polite vocabulary, but he did not comply. His parents, having learned well that attempting to force or consequence Sam usually backfired, provided the creative and supportive alternatives of different phrases he could say or paper versions he could hand to people. But he rarely used these.

Learning from this history, and from observation, that telling Sam what he must do was generally worse than unsuccessful, I chose to meet him where he was and hope we could proceed together. My minimal effort, but consistent involvement, in the first postmaster project suggested that a trusted collaboration would be a huge factor in any further progress.

Together, we set some goals to recover the polite words, planning in the meantime to increase the use of the alternatives his parents offered. It was a hopeful sign when Sam gave Beverly a paper *please* and said, "I'll be glad when I get my polite words back." I tried to say the targeted words frequently but unobtrusively when speaking to him, hoping to point out their usefulness without encouraging him to believe he could magically control other people by saying them.

# MEET ME WHERE I AM

The original vocabulary targets and these social words, all of which were blamed on the postmaster's thievery, were not the full sum of Sam's unique communication habits. He also never said names of foods or first names of people. Sam told me the food words were behind the postmaster's back fence and were unlikely to be recovered before the polite words. Because he would not say the names of foods and had a severely self-limited diet, feeding Sam was somewhat of a challenge. But his father, Stes, said that in some ways it was easy because you only had to prepare the few items that he was unlikely to reject.

There was a particular ritual to the way he would ask for a cookie. It began with Sam standing and staring at the cookies and saying, "I'm hungry." From there, the conversation invariably went like this:

Beverly: (seeing his intent) Then have a cookie.

Samuel: How many?

Beverly: Two.

Samuel: What do I do with them?

Beverly: Eat them.

Whereupon Samuel would happily eat his two cookies. If his mother varied from the ritual, perhaps by saying, "Put them behind your ear" instead of "Eat them," Sam would sit and stare at the cookies indefinitely, and perhaps complain, but he would not eat them.

I remember stopping at Dairy Queen while driving him home from his first visit to my house. Sam could easily read the choices on the menu but could not say which one he wanted. Taken by surprise but knowing that it wasn't going to end well if we now left without ice cream, I had to make a quick decision. So I said, "Do you want A) vanilla, B) twist, or C) chocolate?" to which he cheerfully replied "B!"

The absence of first names was an immediate, and perhaps deliberate, barrier to peer interactions. In first grade at a private school, where Sam preferred the girls because they were more "ruly" than the boys, he had referred to children by spelling their names, including his favorite, C-A-T-H-E-R-I-N-E. He told his mother that he was the second most unruly boy at school.

When I met him, Sam insisted on being called "Samuel" and if I slipped and called him Sam, he would quickly add "uel." He referred to his parents as Momuel and Daduel and referenced other children as "it," possibly to preclude making mistakes about their gender. Since he mostly avoided them anyway, other children were probably not aware that he referred to them as if they were inanimate objects. Adults were referenced by their last names and titles, so I was "Mrs. Field."

Nor would he say the names of items he especially disdained, such as alcohol and tobacco products. In his lexicon these were "objectionable objects."

So, let's see--at age ten, Sam's communication differences included the words he had reinvented because of the postmaster's involvement, the polite and greeting words stolen by the postmaster, and the absent food words, names of "objectionable objects" and first names of people. Was that everything?

Not quite. Sam had an entrenched habit of saying "Don't mumble" every time he heard a non-word vocalization such as *um-hmm, uh-oh, um* or *er*. He would say "Don't mumble!" regardless of whether the offender had been someone he was speaking with or just a person he heard in the background. If a speaker said *um* eleven times in a paragraph, Sam said "Don't mumble" eleven times. But interestingly, he sometimes mumbled himself.

One day when he was eleven and back in school for a while, I was there for a consultation visit. We were in the small glass room that was his private sanctuary at the center of the science lab, which had been repurposed as a learning center.

Sam was sifting sand through his fingers and mumbled an unintelligible sentence with the intonation of a question.

Me: Is something hard to say?

Sam: Why didn't you answer my question?

Me: Because I can't understand it.

Sam: (clearly) Does anybody care about me?

Me: Yes, lots of people care about you. Your teachers do, and I do a great deal, and your parents care more than you can measure.

Sam: (two unintelligible syllables, which could have been a substitute for "Thank you", followed by) "for telling me. Sometimes I'm not sure."

When I told Beverly about this conversation, she said it was one they often had at home. But Sam was twelve before he told his mother that he loved her.

Sam at ten and eleven had advanced vocabulary, excellent grammar and syntax and could spot an error or typo in any written material. Sometimes he insisted on stopping to correct mistakes on bulletin boards and posters. But the vocabulary of emotions often eluded him. When he was eleven, I made him an informal vocabulary quiz containing emotional-relational concepts interspersed with vocabulary from his mother's college psychology text, which he had recently read.

Here is a sample of the results:

Me: Samuel, please define these words.

Coping: "Something that gets you a…what's that word? a rectangle." (He means a ticket toward a reward). "One of the good behaviors in the learning center."

Joyful: "It's another word for happy." (Me: "And what does happy mean?")

"It's very hard for me to do something like that." (Me: "Want to try?")

"NO!"

Retrograde amnesia: "When you forget something because of something that happened after. Like if you had a head injury and forgot what happened before it."

Responsibility: "When you're responsible" (Me: "Can you tell me more?")

"WHEN YOU'RE RESPONSIBLE!" He laughed appreciatively when I responded, "That's not telling me more. That's telling me the same thing louder."

Mmm-hmm: "Don't mumble! It means you're saying something you don't want me to know. Or having a speech problem."

Procedural memory: "That's when you remember how to do something."

Uh-uh: "Don't mumble! It means something else you don't want me to know."

A couple of those answers shed light on why he often said, "Don't mumble."

In a similar quiz involving gestures, Sam did not understand the meaning of a beckoning finger, and he protested, "Don't push me!" when I stepped aside and touched his back to indicate he could go first through a doorway.

Sam was reading before he was three, including words like *symphony* and *cholesterol*. Although he had periods of writing willingly as a young child, he gave it up entirely after being pressured to use a conventional pencil grip and to form letters according to instruction. His refusal to write shut off another potential method of communication.

Like many autistic people, Sam had some intense interests or "enthusiasms" and, at age eleven, he lectured me frequently on subatomic particles. These monologues were a bit disorganized and choppy, and Sam's explanations did not account for my lack of previous knowledge.

He sometimes spoke abruptly to people or said things that might be better left unsaid like commenting loudly that a round lady in a striped bathing suit looked like a beach ball, or interrupting classes to tell teachers their facts were incorrect, or telling my friend Julie, "It must be very difficult being trapped in that small mind of yours."

So, there were plenty of potential goals for a speech language pathologist like me, but I soon learned that his communication differences were entwined with other issues.

# Chapter 3
# And Wait, There's More

Sam's difficulty integrating into life with other people involved more than his unusual communication characteristics. There were multiple other concerns. These were usually rooted in his intense need to avoid any hint that someone else was controlling him and to maintain an environment that was predictable and was proceeding as he felt it should. When things did not go his way, Sam's loud resistance and persistent resolve could disrupt his family or school for a long time. His intolerance for everyday expectations that I called "life realities" and his chosen solutions to them often limited his life and distressed the people who tried to help him. Among the issues were these:

- Sam refused haircuts, saying he had a recessive gene that caused the core of his hair shafts to be alive. Therefore, he reasoned, haircuts were painful to him even though they did not bother other people. He was also loudly and physically resistant to having his long hair combed or washed, insisting that water in his eyes or ears would make him blind or deaf. Toothbrushing was not acceptable either.

- At age ten, he would still not allow his left heel to touch the floor, with or without shoes. He had bumped it on the stairs when he was seven and remained unconvinced when his grandmother gently assured him that he was not injured. Even after an examination by his doctor, and having x-rays that showed no injury, Sam had steadfastly refused to let that heel touch the floor for three years. So far.

- He would wear only solid, brightly colored clothing, including pants and socks, and refused any prints, stripes, or brand logos. He did wear plaid pajamas. Sam would not wear shoes unless they had an extra wide toe box so he could spread his toes apart.

-

# MEET ME WHERE I AM

Because he could not tolerate losing, he would not play a competitive game.

- He would not allow anyone to take his picture.

- If someone touched him, he would panic if the touch was not symmetrical and would insist on the same touch on the other side of his body. He would even chase a stranger who bumped his arm and insist on bumping his other arm against the person.

- "Objectionable objects" must be avoided at all costs, even if it occasionally meant jumping into the street to avoid a cigarette butt on the sidewalk.

- The foods he would eat were very limited and included mostly tan and white carbohydrates and some meats and sweets. He quoted imaginary research explaining why one should not eat green vegetables.

- He avoided stores and most other community activities, especially in inclement weather, refusing to walk five steps from car to house without an umbrella if he spotted one raindrop. He essentially hibernated in the winter, leaving his house infrequently.

- Sam was unable to comply with school expectations that he should do assigned work, wait for a line of children to pass by instead of barging through them, participate calmly in a fire drill, attend classes and specials reliably, let other children answer questions, or tolerate meeting a teacher carrying a lunch tray without fleeing from the building. He felt assaulted by the noise of a fire drill or the smell of cafeteria food, and he did not eat anything at school. Fortunately, he did enjoy taking tests that did not require handwriting, so his teachers were aware of his broad knowledge.

- Most of all, Samuel was very unlikely to do anything that he was directly told to do, and he became incensed if a consequence for his behavior was threatened or imposed.

**So, there were plenty of concerns, but what about strengths?**

Despite all these obstacles to comfortable interaction, no one questioned Sam's intelligence. He demonstrated a great thirst for factual information, a tremendous memory, and a willingness to share his knowledge with others. As a ten-year-old he understood the concepts behind advanced math and science facts, got a *C* on his mother's college psychology test just by reading the textbook, and spent most of his time on independent learning. His persistence and long attention span, which unpleasantly prolonged his emotional upsets, were assets when he was exploring the many topics that interested him.

Sam enjoyed humor, especially puns and other word play, and he studied idioms extensively. When first meeting him, most people were fascinated by Sam's knowledge and quirkiness. But within a few interactions they usually ran afoul of some of his rituals, demands, and refusals, and then had little interest in spending more time with him.

Although he often spoke rudely and had a long memory for incidents that offended him, Sam showed no malice for others. He had no greed for possessions, believed that the government should make sure no one went without necessities, and generally wanted to make the world a better place, possibly with himself in charge. When he corrected his teachers, it was because he felt that the students should know the correct facts, not an attempt to make the teacher look bad. Sam couldn't tolerate an uncorrected error anywhere he saw or heard it.

Another strength was his parent's support as shown through their advocacy at school, attempts to accommodate his needs, appreciation of his intelligence, and desire to help him be happy and successful. Although, of course, they were as challenged by him as everyone was.

**Where did all this come from?**

Sam had diagnoses of Autism and Obsessive-Compulsive Disorder (OCD). He also had an intense antipathy to any sort of external control. Sam was not just demand-avoidant, he also had high expectations of others. He demanded his "needs" instead of requesting his "wants" and he became anxious to the point of panic if his "needs" were not met immediately, or if he was pressured to comply. Compromise was unlikely because Sam feared that if he gave a little, people would then require more. When he and an adult were both determined to prevail, the result was usually a loud and long explosion with no real winners.

Although it was well known that Sam was neurodivergent, much of his behavior was still seen as willful disobedience, and it certainly often appeared to be. It was difficult for people to understand how he could be so intelligent and yet so vehemently opposed to mundane expectations. But people and society often didn't make sense to Sam either, and he had an intense need to make the world safe and comfortable for himself.

Sam was standing squarely at the confluent intersection of autism and OCD; anxious, controlling, and unable to proceed confidently.

**What had been tried?**

Stes and Beverly had enrolled Sam in a preschool that was very accepting of individual differences, and then a Montessori school when it seemed that he wasn't ready for public education. They attempted Cub Scouts, but Sam refused to recite the oath. They explored advanced math instruction, but after meeting Sam the teacher said, "I don't work with disturbed children." They provided many, many books, encouraged him to pursue his interests, and gave him several years of essentially self-directed home schooling. They advocated for accommodations when he was in public school, required baths as infrequently as possible, and cooked foods he would eat. They offered alternatives for things he couldn't do. His mother encouraged a growth mindset by telling Sam that child development was like turning over the cards in a shuffled deck. The things he couldn't do were cards that had not come up yet.

At school, which he attended sporadically, Sam had, of course, an Individual Education Plan (IEP). It included modified expectations, a shorter day, one-to-one assistance which included off-campus swimming, and speech/language and occupational therapies. He attended regular education classes with his aide if he chose to and had a personal retreat space with sensory activities within the special education classroom that was his home base. His teaching team, which also included Sam, his parents, a consulting psychologist and now me, met frequently. At school, there were people who found him extremely aggravating and people who wanted to help him; often they were the same people. Sam was invited to change the principal's wooden daily calendar and she gave him a Hershey Kiss (which he never ate until he left school), even after the day he spit in her face.

Nevertheless, school was very stressful for Sam, and for those around him, and his mother was often called to pick him up early. When upset, his prolonged screams could be heard through much of the building, and he sometimes bolted outdoors. If cornered by a scolding adult, he might strike out. His resistance to any agenda but his own was paramount and he was not prone to compromise or compliance. I remember one incident when a teacher was trying to get Sam to come out of his private room. Because Sam had indicated that he would comply with instructions about safety issues, the adult told him that it wasn't safe for him to be there. He recognized this as illogical and refused to comply, later saying, "If I wasn't safe, they shouldn't have already let me stay there for two hours."

### What next?

With our postmaster project, Sam had demonstrated desire for interaction, support, and recognition...on his terms. He was willing to make changes that could benefit him...again, on his terms. I saw both great potential and tremendous challenges and, having had some early success, wanted to try for more. I hoped that a highly individualized plan, developed with his input, would yield further progress.

Besides, I really liked him.

# Chapter 4

# Samuel Says

Sam, now a young adult, and I have had several conversations that began with me asking, "Why did you need to...?" Often, Samuel initially answered, "I don't know." But after a brief reflection, he would speculate that there was likely an incident in which he balked or protested, an adult insisted, and he resisted. Thus began a pattern in which he resisted more firmly with each insistence until his refusal was stone wall solid. Over time, even mild expectations became a threat to his self-determination and his *can't/won't/mustn'ts* expanded.

He says the postmaster problem may have developed from people correcting his mispronunciations or misarticulations of words. Because Sam read on many topics well beyond those he would be exposed to conversationally, it is quite likely that he could read many words he did not know how to pronounce. However, once he had decided how the word should be pronounced, he would have been loath to change it from the form familiar to him. I remember that he insisted that the Biblical Job should be pronounced the same as the *job* meaning employment. After all, the man's name doesn't end with a silent *e*.

Sam remembers once asking his mother a question and expecting a *yes* answer. When she responded with *uh-huh* or *mmhmm*, he demanded that she say the word *yes*. He sees this as the beginning of a belief that when people used expressions like *uh-huh, mmhmm, uh-uh* and *uh-oh* they were either being deliberately annoying or trying to keep him from understanding. He could have made a study of these expressions and readily learned their meanings, as he did with idioms, but instead he began to say "Don't mumble" every time he heard one.

Given his resistance to adult insistence, it is pretty easy to see why he stopped saying *please, thank you* and other adult-prompted words. Also, these -and greetings- are purely social words that often seem irrelevant or confusing to autistic children.

Young children, especially those with autism, often resist the sensory invasiveness of hygiene procedures like toothbrushing and hair combing or washing, and parents may be required to insist. Although Bev and Stes tried to be understanding and accommodating, they were not able to make Sam completely comfortable with these procedures, so he felt the need to absolutely prohibit them. He was so noisy during baths and shampoos that his parents wondered if the neighbors might call child protective services.

He thinks his requirement for bright colored, no pattern, clothing started as a preference and became an iron-clad rule after his mother tried to introduce some neutral colors or other variations. She ended up making red, yellow, or lime green pants for him when bright colored ones were no longer available in his size. I remember discovering a stray pair of red carpenter pants on a bargain rack. Sam exclaimed, "These look like they were made just for me!" Apparently, they were, 'cause no one else had wanted them.

He didn't know the origin of his symmetry need but said there was a precursor; he became upset if he traveled somewhere in a car and came home by a different route.

Keeping his left heel from touching the floor resulted directly from the single incident of bumping it on the stairs and then denying his grandmother's assurance that it was not injured. He believes that seven years went by before he allowed that heel to touch the floor or ground, with or without a shoe. When I asked, "Did you put it down sometimes when you were alone, and no one would know?" Sam replied, "I don't believe so. It stayed clean."

Sam told me recently, "I didn't have the vocabulary" to explain his many issues and concerns, and "I was stubborn," leading to this conversation:

Me: I'm surprised to hear you call yourself stubborn. I remember that you always became very angry if anyone referred to you with a negative adjective like stubborn or lazy.

Sam: I saw those words as blaming me, labeling a defect. But now, I just am.

Me: So, do you consider stubbornness a neutral characteristic now?

Sam: Yes. It's okay because I can't change it and wouldn't.

Sam is a firm believer in having the courage of one's convictions, even if others call it stubbornness.

At age ten he was especially determined not to concede defeat about anything he resisted or demanded. To do so would reinforce the efforts of the offending adults and make them more inclined to insist in other situations. Samuel says he learned this from adults telling him they couldn't give in to his noisy demands because doing so would reinforce his undesired behavior.

**And what about school?**

Sam still harbors feelings of resentment about his elementary education. Even when I point out the many accommodations the school made for him, he says:

"The school should meet the needs of all the students. If I could tell my fifth and sixth grade self about school, I would say, 'This probably isn't going to work out. You might as well do home schooling until high school.' But I never refused to go to school. If I wasn't there it was their choice, not mine."

"So," said I, "Are you saying that you were not part of the problem?"

He promptly replied, "Mu!" meaning that's an invalid question. "The schools are responsible for making it work. It's their entire raison d'etre. Schools exist for the students. Students do not exist for the schools."

"But would you agree they tried to help?"

"Some of their efforts were to help me and some were to force me. They regarded me as a thing. They approached me as a malfunctioning widget!"

**I say…**

Sam and I discussed my desire to include a section of my viewpoints in this chapter, and he approved it as "adding context from your experience." We agreed that chapters including his viewpoints and mine would end with a "last word" from Samuel.

It frequently appeared that Sam's maladaptive behaviors were rooted in his need to control others and to not yield to others' expectations. But I believe that his control compulsions grew from anxiety. He was living with an unusual sort of brain in a confusing world where the other inhabitants set different priorities, interacted in mysterious ways, and could tolerate, or even enjoy, noise, smells, and touch that he found noxious.

## MEET ME WHERE I AM

So, viewing anxiety as a significant contributor to the problems, and believing that trust was a potent antidote to anxiety, I tried, within the limits of my experience and patience, to provide low-pressure, collaborative support focused on Sam's individual situation.

Some things that seemed to help so far:

- Recognizing that his beliefs and actions were consistent and absolute, and that he would be even less likely to change if told that he should or must.

- Avoiding confrontations, directives or consequences and trying to find a solution when his "issues" caused a roadblock (like at the Dairy Queen).

- Accepting the postmaster as the reality Sam could share, empathizing with his problem ("You deserve to have your words") and inviting his participation in finding a solution. But trying not to enhance or expand the postmaster scenarios.

- Appreciating, but not pushing, the slow, steady word recovery project. Accepting the limits he set ("no polite words").

- Enjoying informal time with Sam in which he led the activities and I learned to know and like him even better.

**The Last Word:**

Sam still feels strongly about being controlled and has hypothesized a new personality disorder representing a pathological need to control others. He suggests naming it Authoritarian Personality Disorder, Kyriopathic Personality Disorder, or Archopathic Personality Disorder and says that people with this condition should not be allowed to work in education, law enforcement or middle management. And parenting should be allowed only with supervision.

# Chapter 5

# In and Out of School

When Sam and I met to discuss the postmaster, he was ten years old. Over several decades, I had known and liked many autistic children and teens, but there was something about Sam and his parents that resonated with me immediately. As we navigated through the postmaster project, Sam impressed me as earnest, determined, and willing to consider alternatives if encouraged but not pressured. His parents were supportive and eager to help him but had become disappointed and distrustful of the school system's efforts. They felt that they were seen as part of the problem.

## In School

In September, Samuel turned eleven and returned to his elementary school as a sixth grader with a partial day schedule and a one-to-one tutor. I was then a consultant to his school district, for Sam and several other students. All of the issues described in Chapters 2, 3 and 4 were in full force.

Samuel, his speech/language pathologist, and I agreed on some goals for communication and classroom participation. During that school year, Sam completed the original postmaster project from Chapter 1, did a classroom presentation as part of his school speech and language program, made more phone calls to me, taught a study hall art class with his mother, and began to contemplate getting back nine polite/social words.

Within his modified day, the school provided regular education for reading, social studies, and computer, individualized special education and guidance sessions, occupational therapy, speech/language therapy, psychological services, adaptive physical education, the tutor, my consultation, and the opportunities to teach art lessons with his mother and to swim at the local YMCA with a family friend. But all did not go smoothly.

Sam struggled with the noise, smells, and confusion of a busy school, with his tutor's variations between friendly joking and firmer authority, with the rules he felt should be enforced for others, and with the expectations and consequences that he could not accept as applying to himself. He attended his own IEP and team meetings, sometimes pacing around the table in circles. Once, when the conference room telephone rang, Sam picked it up and yelled, "We're trying to have a meeting in here!"

In my consultant role, I observed that he was easily upset by classroom noise and would shout, "This class is too noisy!" or "Why don't you all sit down now!" One day, I encouraged him to attend his adaptive physical education session with me, and later commented that he had had a good time. Sam looked surprised and replied, "I did?" In science lab, where he refused his tutor's attempts to get him to participate, I said I would do the project if he would tell me how to do it. Before the end, he had recognized that he could do better than I was doing and started assembling the electromagnet. As we left the class, his science teacher commented that this was the most he had participated.

After receiving a three-day suspension for hitting his tutor and his computer teacher when they pressured him to go to class, Sam was distraught to learn that Saturday and Sunday did not count toward the three days. He asked, "Why can't they cool off over the weekend?" This was the year he spit at the principal because she said she was trying to treat him like all the other students. Sam did not think he was like the other students, but he did adamantly believe that he deserved a free education.

Another problem at school was Sam's habit of standing still in the hall and screaming if he happened to get bumped by a person or object. He and I discussed a plan to address this without the screams, but Sam insisted, "That cannot happen because it's impossible. I have to make noise and it has to be loud." So, we settled on a "step in the right direction" involving props and reinforcers for walking to the Learning Center as he screamed instead of standing still. He was willing to try this until the school added a consequence for the screaming and he abandoned the whole plan.

Before the school year ended, Samuel was not attending any regular education classes and the tutor was gone. But he did score in the 99th percentile on state achievement testing.

# MEET ME WHERE I AM

**Out of school**

In the Spring of his sixth-grade year, Sam and I began working more often at his house and expanded our goals to include a wider range of issues and new methods to approach them. Typically, I wrote the goals and either Sam approved them, sometimes grudgingly, or I dropped them until later. I had drafted a goal that he would demonstrate any two activities from a collection of "life realities" on three different occasions. The options were line waiting, hair cutting, losing a game, accepting clothing variations, ordering food, eating a new food, eating in a different place, or being photographed. He thoroughly inked out this goal on my paper, so I did not include it on his IEP. But after discussion with Sam, I reported to the team that "These are of such intense importance to Sam that he was unwilling to include any as specific objectives, but he understands that I will be gently nudging him toward greater flexibility in these areas." A key premise of our work together was that I would not try to force him to change, but that I would keep trying to help him change things that would make his life better.

Around this time, Sam expressed an approach-avoidance desire to see my home in a nearby city. So, after I drew him a floor plan of the downstairs and upstairs to minimize surprises, he and his mother followed me home. I remember he had asked his grandmother if they could borrow her car, and when she agreed he "thanked" her three times in American Sign Language and then ran to get one of his printed *Thank you* papers to give her. We toured my house and neighborhood and, despite some alarm at meeting my teenage son, Ryan, and his friends, Sam decided he would like to come again by himself.

As we spent longer times together in more places, which eventually included my family's summer home on a coastal island, there were more opportunities to address the many concerns of Chapters 1, 2 and 3.

**The Process:**

Although our visits were anchored in enjoying each other's company and doing ordinary things, there were goals and agendas involved.

As mentioned, many of our formally stated goals were either preapproved by Sam or not written into IEPs. Sometimes the goal-related plan for a particular visit would be discussed when he arrived, especially if an activity I proposed was new or potentially stressful. Other times, our plan would just flow naturally. But there were always goals, especially in the areas of communication and interaction, life skills, and community involvement.

We approached our goals with a combination of:

<u>Multiple discussions</u>: These often ended with Sam shouting, "I don't want to discuss it!" and me saying "Okay, but I'll probably bring it up again sometime."

<u>Gradual approximation and role-playing:</u> We did pretend haircuts, drive-bys and location photos before community visits, and we practiced taking phone messages. We made miniature people go places and do things that Sam could not. Sometimes I just started a refused activity so he could see how it went before joining.

<u>Supportive adaptations:</u> These included building in alone time for recovery from hours of interaction, providing sensory squeezing and squashing, always having food he would eat, leaving if he said he needed to go from a public place, avoiding confrontation, and staying calm myself when he wasn't.

<u>Deals with reinforcement</u> His favorite reinforcer was Together Time, in which Sam got to decide what we would do for an

earned period of time. This provided motivation but also gave him an acceptable face-saving reason to agree to something he had initially and automatically refused to do.

<u>Practicing in real settings</u> Nearly everything we did occurred in a natural setting or at home preparing for the real-world experience. Many times, we went places for an errand or other purpose but also so we could practice.

When Sam was 11 and 12 years old, there was a lot going on in the arenas of communication, "life realities," and community involvement. Here is some of it:

**Communication:** Shortly after we celebrated the return of all the ordinary words stolen by the postmaster, Sam told me that he was going to babysit so the postmaster could clean house and look for the key to the dead letter office where the polite words were locked. Sam tended "the postmaster's four-year-old child," the postmaster found the key, but the polite words did not return. Sam did sometimes say "I'm grateful...," "I appreciate...," "I apologize..." and even, "I am grateful that you are grateful." But six months later, there were still no common polite words or greetings.

Sam negotiated with me an expensive deal in which he would earn one hour of Together Time if he used one polite word once. We made a list of nine polite words or phrases and he numbered them according to the order in which he would like to get them back. They were *please, thank you, excuse me, I'm sorry, you're welcome, hello/hi, goodbye/bye, good morning, good night.* He seemed especially interested in getting back the word *please*, which made me wonder if he was thinking it might help him avoid an unpleasant dental event that was looming. Eventually he practiced silently mouthing the nine words in random order, and my job was to guess and say them aloud.

At a visit with his psychologist in December I told Sam that no one could take his words anymore now that he was 12 years old, and he said "Okay." I followed up with a letter reminding him that no one could take his words, since he has backup copies that he can use whenever he wants, and that no one should tell him what he must say. If someone does try to tell him he must say something, he might be annoyed or angry, but he will still be able to use those words any other time he wants them.

On Christmas Eve that year, Sam was unexpectedly at my home while Bev and Stes took Bev's mother, "Ninu" to Sam, to the emergency room. I asked if he could say one polite word as a Christmas gift for me. After some delay while he imposed an impossible guess-the-number game on me, Sam took a deep breath and said all nine polite words from our list.

First names also appeared during that Christmas season. A couple of weeks before Christmas he had been arranging my creche by putting the baby Jesus in a back corner of the stable with everyone else facing out and clustered protectively around the baby, and he began to use their names instead of referring to "the baby's mother" and so on.

On Christmas Eve, after I mentioned that Jesus wasn't as afraid of people as Sam was at that time, he rearranged them so that Mary, Joseph and the wisemen were turned to look at Jesus, but they were all still at the back of the stable and blocking any live person's view of the baby. He again referred to them by their names. Before he went home that night, he was calling me and my family by our first names.

# Chapter 6
# Life Happens

And sometimes a lot of life happens at the same time. That was true for Samuel the year he was twelve.

**Teeth**

Shortly before Sam turned twelve, we learned he might need to have several teeth pulled. He immediately initiated an avoidance campaign, saying he would need "49, No! 7×49" opinions and that I should help him get out of it. I explained it was his parents' decision, but I would support him as much as possible if he needed to do it.

The next month, after an anxious huddle in the oral surgeon's waiting room and a collapse onto the floor between his father and me when called in to the consult, Sam tolerated a brief examination.

Then there was a brief lull until a month later when Sam learned the appointment for his surgery was in two weeks. He insisted, rather frantically, that he had other obligations that day. But when I said this surgery would indeed happen on November 4th, and I would help all I could, he rescheduled his "other obligations" to December 8th three years later at precisely 10:28:34628439746283982643 am, his "next available date."

On October 28th, Sam, Stes and I went to a pre-admission session at the hospital. Sam was extremely anxious, shouting, "Don't let people get near me!" but after some hugs and my promise that "I can't control them going by, but I will stand in front of you if you need me to" he calmed enough to meet with the nurse and anesthesiologist. He alternated between asking them questions and hopping up to whack at them with a rolled-up hospital brochure, but he did let me sit him down repeatedly. They agreed that he could wear new pajamas instead of a johnny and that his blood pressure could be taken after he was asleep. We had a recovery visit at my house after this appointment. Every time November 4th was mentioned

Sam would throw himself on the floor retching, but he was able to discuss the process somewhat.

A couple of days later we practiced mouth rinses and eating Jell-O. The dramatic response to hearing "November 4$^{th}$" was receding.

Sam arrived at my home, a few blocks from the hospital, at 2:30 pm on November 3rd to stay overnight before his oral surgery. He was fairly calm through the evening and his parents brought takeout for supper. He said he planned to try to stay asleep through the whole process the next day and I offered a minute-for-minute Together Time for no running and no fighting at the hospital. Sam accepted the offer and had a last snack at 11:30. He was very conscientious about no food or water after midnight though he stayed up until 1:30 am.

Bev and Stes arrived at 6:15 am and Stes carried Sam to the car, to the accompaniment of a few brief screams. At the hospital he stayed wrapped in blankets in a wheelchair trying hard to be asleep through an hour of interviewing and waiting. He transferred to a gurney without fuss, let me put the operating room hat on him and grinned at mine. In the OR he shrieked and fought the mask screaming "It smells bad!" I counted down from 100 and Sam was asleep at 87. The extractions were successful, and the oral surgeon saved the removed teeth for him.

I rejoined Sam in the recovery room before he woke muttering, "Don't mumble." Then he shrieked until his IV was out and yanked at his blood pressure cuff. He soon resisted letting any nurse into the room, so his father held the stethoscope on Sam's chest while the nurse timed it from beyond the threshold. Even on the way to the car he was screaming, "Don't let anyone get near me!" We all stayed at my house until 11:30, his parents left, and Stes returned with sherbet. Bev, Stes and Sam's grandmother, Ninu, came back again for dinner with my family and took him home.

Sam's mouth recovered uneventfully, but his anxiety spiked significantly after this oral surgery and he became extremely fearful of being anywhere near people, their cups, or their coats.

## Medication

After two months on a waiting list, Sam got an appointment at our regional psychiatric hospital two weeks after his oral surgery. He went willingly but needed help dealing with his fear of other people in the waiting room and halls. Mostly, he played on the office floor mat, after protesting that the map was a road, and the toys were train pieces not cars. He kept his back to the psychiatric nurse and psychiatrist as they interviewed his parents at length and was stressed by smells from a nearby microwave, but he left more calmly than he had arrived. A major antipsychotic medication was prescribed, and Sam said he would need "six weeks to think about it."

Meanwhile, our work together included recurring discussions of his fear of cups, coats, and people and possible accommodations and plans we could try. I explained again that I could not/would not control other people even in my family. Sam adjusted his tendency to just scream out what he needed. As he struggled to pass my son Ethan in the hall, he was able to negotiate with him to move aside, saying, "I'd really appreciate..." and "I'm grateful that..." This was before the ordinary polite words, *please* and *thank you* were recovered.

We started a reference book of emotion words like *proud* and *worried* and talked about his worries and things his parents might worry about. I told him he didn't need to call all of his requests "needs." I said I was willing to grant "wants" too and that he deserved to have some wants. There were small triumphs like Sam being able to arrive at my house by the side door and leave by the front door or putting on socks he had previously worn for a few minutes.

Sam's parents, Sam, and I had little enthusiasm about the proposed antipsychotic medication, and it had not been tried when we went to his second appointment two weeks later. Sam was extremely distressed by other people in the waiting room that day, screaming loudly and trying to bolt. After discussion, the psychiatrist changed his prescription to a starter dose of the SSRI Luvox. At my house later, we worked on pill-taking by swallowing mini-M&Ms, talked about the possible benefits of medication, and did a lot of sensory-based play like crawling through a stretchy cloth tube or being caught and squeezed. One day, Sam inhibited an impulse to squeal about mugs on the table and I praised him--later.

On a Saturday about a month after Sam's new prescription, I went to his house because Bev said she felt he was getting close to taking the medication. I had told him he could come for an overnight on Sunday if he had taken the pill by then, so he planned to wait until Sunday morning. I told him I would take him now for both nights if he took the pill today. We all spent a long time sitting in the Stessel's kitchen trying to get the pill swallowed. Sam made many attempts but could not quite drop it into his mouth. Then he suggested crushing it in ice cream as his guidance counselor had told him she did for her daughter. Bev and Stes crushed the pill, and prepared three spoonfuls of ice cream, one hiding the crushed pill. Sam ate all the ice cream, tasted the pill, shuddered, and wolfed down some M&Ms. Leaving with me a few minutes later, he said that one problem had already disappeared – "I don't need someone between me and the back of the driveway." I had never known that this was a concern. I asked if he was happy he took the pill. Sam replied, "In the words of that little boy, (an eleven-year-old mentioned by his psychiatrist) I'm happy I'm getting my life back." Sam stuck pretty close to me that weekend, ate less than usual, wanted lots of deep pressure squashing and did not leave the house at all, but he was able to wait briefly when I cooked, helped someone, or spoke on the phone.

This was around the time that he first rearranged my nativity set and started calling Mary, Joseph and Jesus by name. He also made up a name for a toy boy, now "Robert," that we often used in imaginary play about medication, hiding vitamins, hospital tests and eating habits.

There was no pill Saturday night because Sam had taken the first one in the midafternoon, but on Sunday morning he balked. I had to tell him "My job now is to help you take the pill. I can't play until it's done." I put myself "on pause" and sat alone by the pill for 25 to 30 minutes. Then with some more encouragement and the three-spoon ice cream roulette, he took it. There were some medication ups and downs, but within a few months Sam was taking the Luvox, and Benadryl at bedtime, reliably.

**Ninu**

Sadly, Ninu's Christmas Eve emergency room visit resulted in the diagnosis of advanced breast cancer and she lived only another three months. During that time, Sam firmly refused to discuss her illness, though he did wait to let me visit her and sometimes asked me to request prayers for her at church. Sam chronically avoided discussing stressful topics, but he was especially adamant about this one. One time, playing with miniature people, he told me that I was not allowed to bring up stressful topics if I saw a yellow man with a yellow hat in a yellow boat, and then proceeded to drive that toy directly to me. More often he just shouted, "Don't talk about stresses! Always stop when I say stop!"

One day, he came across my mother-in-law's living will file and asked about it. I explained that it contained her choices about end-of-life care and when she would want people to stop trying to keep her alive. Sam said he would want all efforts made to keep him alive. I asked, "But what should we do if others don't want that? Should we respect their wishes?" He said that we should if they were conscious but otherwise, we should keep them alive. So I said, "Well if Ninu..." and he cut me off with "I don't want to talk about it anymore." I believe that he knew she was dying but did not want it said out loud.

When Ninu did die early on the morning of March 23, Bev called, and I went to be there with Sam while his parents made the necessary arrangements. Sam was still in bed when they told him, and he responded by pulling the covers over his head and whimpering. His parents left to make important calls. When I reminded Sam that Ninu's death was not his fault and he could not have prevented it, he pulled his head out and eventually walked shakily and shuddery to the bathroom. We went to Ninu's apartment over their attached garage where Sam sat by her bed and asked about her illness. He touched her and rested on the other side of her bed. We talked about the coming removal of the body Ninu no longer needed, and the planned cremation. Sam wanted to use the controls on the rented hospital bed but agreed to wait until the bed was empty. He kissed his grandmother's forehead and said "I love you. Goodbye." Several times that day he asked me "How did you feel when I said, 'Don't discuss stressfuls!'" I replied that it made me sad and worried because I wanted to help him deal with it so today wouldn't be quite so hard. But that it was OK, I understood. Bev, Stes, and I all told him several times that Ninu's death was not his fault, and that he did much to make her last weeks happier by holding her hand, giving her kisses, reading her Bible stories, telling her he loved her and beginning to have haircuts.

He needed to hear several times that she would not have lived one more day if he had not hit her on the breast when he was four years old. We talked about disease, death, unhappiness, God, and research. Sam said that if we hadn't wasted time with wars, we might have more disease cures. He understood that his grandmother, a devout Christian Scientist, was not afraid of death and looked forward to an afterlife. But he reminded me that he would never want a Living Will and he insisted on my "promise" that he would live a long time.

During our visits later that month, Sam often brought up discussions of Ninu, asking how I felt when he refused to discuss it before her death. He wanted to know why I hadn't told him the name of her illness, saying, "Is that because I wouldn't let you get far enough?"

He expressed concern that his hits might have caused "cells to start dividing," and needed frequent reassurance that Ninu's illness was not his fault.

**Church**

In January, after the November oral surgery and December pill-taking, and during Ninu's illness, Sam decided he might go to church with me. First, we visited the empty church, and studied the bulletin and I described all the steps of the service. On his first Sunday, Sam chose to sit at the center-aisle end of the back pew with me beside him, and for some unexplainable reason, three different ushers tried to cut through in front of us. Sam was very alarmed and tried to flee, but recovered each time, and the ushers learned to stay out of our pew. He studied the program, sat, and listened, leaning on me, and shuddering occasionally. He tried to put my check in the offering plate but panicked, dashed into the aisle, and came back. After about 40 minutes, he wanted to leave, but was able to wait until the prayer ended. Back at my house, he looked up the scripture and read it, then played with the manger set, mixing in a tollbooth game as he helped the holy family flee to Egypt. Later, listening to a tape of the service, he smiled and shook hands with himself while hearing the recorded break for greetings. He told me what he was doing and said, "It's a start." Given his significant people phobia, shaking hands with somebody else was pretty unlikely.

Going to church was our first frequently repeated community "excursion" and provided a forgiving environment for some new experiences. Bev said that Sam listened to the tapes of the church services every night for a while, and he told me that he was singing along with the hymns. Eventually he tolerated me singing them at church and sometimes even joined in. His people fear was in high gear at this time, and we sometimes had to walk into church with his eyes closed and me leading him. And more than once he shouted, "Please stay as far away as possible!" at people nearby. I told him he could close his eyes and lean on me if he was anxious and reminded him that this was a safe place with good people, saying, "I have been here a lot and you don't need to be afraid if I am not." His shrieks and shuddering subsided with familiarity, and he sometimes marched in ahead of me if I paused to speak to someone.

Gradually we moved closer to the front of the church because he wanted to better see what was going on. He would not sit in the 13th row and did not want anyone else in a pew with us. I suggested we might as well sit in the very front row because not many people wanted to sit there. He began to go to the front of the church for the children's message but maintained a considerable distance from other children.

Sam asked me to explain his issues to the congregation during the "Joys and Concerns" segment of the service and later, to request prayers for Ninu. After about three months of fairly regular attendance, Sam announced that he had a joy: "I had very severe OCD, but it has improved significantly." He began to shake hands with me during the greeting and later with one or two other people. And he sometimes wanted to chat with the pastor about the sermon. We worked hard at not making comments, asking questions, or correcting people during the church service. Sam felt the congregation needed to know that a speaker had mentioned the wrong century or made an error on some other fact but finally accepted telling me quietly rather than loudly interrupting. I also discovered that discussing on the way to church what he might say during "Joys and Concerns" could save me from some cringeworthy moments during the service.

When the next Christmas rolled around, Sam, now thirteen, wanted to bring his parents to the Christmas Eve service with my family. He was pleased that we filled a pew, so none of the many strangers could join us, and he proudly showed his parents around the church saying, "I wanted you to see my church." Sam and I had also gone to church on Christmas Sunday, but he insisted that we leave early after I had foolishly teased him that it sounded like a sermon he should hear. The title was "Giving Up Control."

## Chapter 7
# Excursions and Discussions

Getting out into the world became more difficult after the stresses of oral surgery and the resulting explosion of Sam's fear of people and personal things they use, such as cups, napkins, and coats. This was also the stressful time of Ninu's advancing illness. Sam still wanted to come to my house, church, the island, a bookstore, and libraries.

So, we focused on maintaining the accepted outings and trying to add brief stops inside McDonald's or Dairy Queen, but mostly he vigorously negotiated for drive-thru. He did go into Dairy Queen to order an ice cream cake for his father's birthday, with his hood up and sticking close to me. He even wrote out for the clerk how to spell "Daduel." It was momentous because at that time Sam was never writing and rarely talking to unfamiliar people. Having a solid counter between him and store clerks did make those interactions a bit easier.

After thoroughly studying the floor plan, he agreed to several trips to explore the mall, once even suggesting we go there "to satisfy your excursion needs."

But grocery stores were impossible because they sold those "objectionable objects," cigarettes and alcohol. One day he really wanted a cake from the grocery store but simply could not go in. So, we compromised. Sam waited between the automatic doors dodging customers while I grabbed and bought the cake. But it was not until eleven months later that he called me to announce excitedly, "There's been a budget cut in the phobia department of my brain" and went to the grocery store with his parents.

We managed to add visits to a coffee shop after church a few times, at first just sticking our heads in to count the booths. Sam typically chose a booth near the door because he "might need to escape." As we left one day, the waitress called, "Come in again" and Sam asked, "Why is she ordering us to come in again?" I explained it was an invitation to return another day, not an order. Sam said "Oh!" and stepped back through the door, grinning and saying, "I came in again."

School at this time was occasional home tutoring with the school guidance counselor or one of two tutors hired to work with him at home or school. But despite their patient efforts and some early hopeful signs, neither tutor worked out long term. We did go to school to see some therapists and attend his team meetings, with Sam squealing, dashing off, or diving under a table if people came too near him. Just getting to the school usually required a bribe of Together Time afterwards. In the second half of this seventh-grade year, we visited the computer lab and social studies once a week, with some degree of success. Of course, he wouldn't sit next to another student at a computer, so I squeezed in between them. He tended to fuss about his peers' behaviors and believed he should be called on for every answer in social studies. One day, he tried to accomplish this by raising his hand, extended with a yardstick, or while standing on his chair. Nevertheless, the computer teacher mentioned on two occasions that Sam had improved a lot.

Sam had not allowed anyone to take a picture of him since he was six years old, and he resisted a lot of my proposals about photography. I gave him a camera the summer he was twelve and, for a while, he took pictures of objects but not people. Then one day in August, he called me to say I could take pictures of him at his house. He hoped it would "inspire Momuel to stop smoking."

We started with a picture of him, not visible, inside the caboose in his back yard, then two of him inside a stretchy cloth tunnel with only his shape showing. I said "Smile!" and Sam snorted, "Very funny!" Next, I took two pictures of him in a mask and then about fifteen more of Sam posed around different parts of his home with no mask. Later, he agreed to have his eighth-grade school picture done while I told him a familiar joke. The joke was about a pilot's wife asking the pilot how he could find Detroit at midnight in a snowstorm but couldn't find the salt on his own kitchen table. At the pilot's punchline, "Well, they don't move Detroit," Sam, who had heard and told the joke many times, laughed enthusiastically. We got a great picture.

Sam went with his parents and me to a summer picnic at his old preschool that year, but he spent much of it in a small back room exploring some toys. When I helped him pick up and asked who was going to carry out the big box of toys, Sam replied, "a cell with a nucleus" which I correctly interpreted as "eukaryote—you carry it." And I did. But Sam was beginning to carry his own belongings more often and one island day that summer he hand-carried a live lobster a mile home from the dock.

At twelve, Sam usually insisted on holding my hand near streets, but on the island traffic was lighter and the lobstermen's rattly old trucks announced their presence well in advance of their arrival. There, he traveled more freely on foot and on his training wheel bike. With his left heel still not touching the ground, he left 1 ½ footprints as he ran barefoot in the low-tide sand.

He still protested leaving the island house to visits to friends and shops, asking, "Why do you need so many excursions?" After outings, even the few he spontaneously suggested, Sam required lots of recovery time playing alone, playing with me, doing puzzles, requesting sensory activities, and lecturing me on science topics. During one jigsaw puzzle session I announced, "I think these are the ears of my deer," and Sam grinned, flapped his ears and said, "Do you mean these?"

He especially loved, and was emotionally soothed by, replaying familiar scripts we had created either as role play or with miniature people and accessories. Most of these related to somewhat controversial events in his life such as hiding vitamins, school upsets, and travel fears. We replayed these scenarios many times, and only one of us got bored. When I tried to change the outcome, as a teaching tool or just for variety or to be mischievous, Sam would accuse me of "cast mutiny."

Deep pressure sensory activities also reduced his tension and helped him relax. Favorites included being made into a Sam sandwich between two couch cushions with me pushing down on the top, or pretending to be a noisy Awk-bird and being tightly caught in a blanket wrap, or having me squeeze his joints together to assemble him into a Sam doll. One day he initiated a trust game of having me catch his head before he slammed it into the floor. He had an approach-avoidance conflict about hugs, often telling me I gave him too many, but then actively seeking them when I agreed to stop hugging for a specific length of time or until he had said the same phrase seven times in a row.

---

We talked about a lot of issues during our extended times together, sometimes as they happened, like the day he dropped a beanbag chair on my cat and sat down in the beanbag. I was alerted by the muffled meows, rescued Micah and, with my arm around Sam, expressed my concern for the cat's welfare. Sam had just been playing, and he was distressed by my reaction. He said I had hurt his neck, to which I replied, "It's not your neck, it's your feelings that hurt." He recited a variation of a familiar theme, "You should never hurt my feelings no matter what bad things I do."

More often, I initiated discussions later, when the behavioral crisis had passed. Topics included acceptable behavior in church and other public places, how people in videos were feeling, missing Ninu, my family's need for some of my attention during his visits, recent situations for which he might need to make apologies, how to heal his left heel, his anxious need to establish a reset after a confrontation, the "people problem", conflicts with his parents, immediate goals, concerns for his future, the "evenness need," how others would respond to impulsive aggressions as he got bigger, and his life-restricting control issues.

And, of course, there were confrontations. We had some standoffs about eating sugar out of the bowl, or sneaking sweets, or wanting to climb too high in a tree, needing to brush his teeth, take a shower or go to a school meeting, and so on, but we got through them all somehow. Sometimes the solution was a Together Time deal, sometimes an explanation ("I'd rather you be angry at me for not helping you climb higher than hurt yourself falling out of the tree) occasionally a stern admonition (to which Sam once responded, "Don't be like the back of a boat!") and very rarely, a threat.

That happened one day when he was peeling the bark off the island birch trees and just peeled faster when I asked him to stop, so I pulled him away from the trees and he screamed and dashed back to peel more when I let him go. Then he started frantically flying around pulling up flowers and I threatened, "If you can't get settled, I'll have to take you home." Sam stopped in shock and demanded, "Don't threaten!" He insisted several times for a promise that I would not punish him for any bad behavior. Knowing that any sort of consequence was a trigger for his control anxiety, I explained that although life does involve consequences, I wouldn't punish him, but that I did need ways to help him get in control of himself. Usually, we managed this with downtime breaks, sensory activities, deals, and calm explanations. Sam stopped tearing up the yard that day, but he was twitchy, needed lots of hugs and reassurance that evening, and called me to sit by his bed four times between 11:30 pm and 4:00 am.

---

In addition to his allergy to consequences, Sam was resistant to praise for deliberate positive behavior or self-control. When I said I was proud of him for not collapsing on a long hot walk, he retorted, "You shouldn't have any good feeling when I'm uncomfortable." And when I admired his self-control for avoiding the bathroom that contained Ryan's shaving cream (because he had squirted it all over the room at an earlier visit) he said, "Don't talk about it!" It seemed that he heard my comment not as approval but as a reminder of a past misdemeanor. Or perhaps he was anxious from recognizing that he needed, and actually was trying, to control himself.

Knowing that Sam wanted to fix the world so it would work smoothly for everyone, I asked him if he (as person A) would give up something he wanted to benefit someone else (person B).

He said that he, A, wouldn't do for another, B, if it meant sacrifice for him, but the other, B, should do for him. So I asked, "What would you think if you were an observer, C. He believed that if he was neither A nor B, then both A and B should be willing to sacrifice something for the other, adding, "Listen, there are two absolutes. The speed of light and I will generally try to get what I want."

"Well," I sighed, "I guess the 'generally' part is progress." We discussed the "aut" of autism as meaning "self" and that much of the world thinks more like person C which could lead to people resenting him and seeing him as selfish.

Stressful discussions, like excursions, necessitated familiar ritual games afterwards. Many of the discussion topics focused on social behavior and Sam scratched the words *social* and *challenges* off my business card as the "two most stressful words."

One day, playing in the family room, Sam made a circle of pick-up sticks around himself as a fortress. It reminded me of a poem by Edwin Markham:

He drew a circle that shut me out—

Heretic, rebel, a thing to flout.

But Love and I had the wit to win:

We drew a circle that took him in!

He asked me to explain the meaning and then asked me to recite it about 20 more times, insisting, "It doesn't have the same feeling when I say it in my head."

---

I was pretty scrupulous about keeping any promises I made, like leaving public places as soon as he asked, prodding but not forcing progress, always being truthful, not trying to trick him, helping him through things he couldn't avoid, and assuring him I would protect him from danger at all costs, but Sam still felt the need to test me. Sometimes we left public places because he was anxious, alarmed or overwhelmed, but other times he was just bored or testing me. And there were lots of little tests.

*Why should I wear that shirt?*

*Well, it looks better than this one but wear this one if you want.*

*You passed the test. I'll wear that one.*

When I didn't protest that he refused to remove his glasses to sleep one night, Sam said, "I guess I can take them off since I'm in control. That was a test. You got an A-."

Once, after a long day when Sam spoke to me in an extra-demanding voice I complained, "That makes me feel devalued" to which he replied, "You are highly valued." Acknowledgements like this, and once, "Where would I be without you?" were rare but they meant a lot to me. If we had a significant conflict, he would often ask if I still loved him. I always reassured him, and he once said, "I love you too, no matter how many things you make into lessons."

# MEET ME WHERE I AM

After about six months, the people problem had faded greatly but Sam's "evenness need" for symmetrical touch on both sides of his body was rampant. And he wanted it met immediately, telling me, "I need to know my evenness need is more important than what you are doing." He imposed this rule on everyone, even total strangers. Even the cat.

Sam had other rules. According to him, Rule #1 was, "If it makes me unhappy, even a tiny bit, I can't get any benefit from the experience."

He still felt compelled to say "don't mumble" when he heard a vocalization like "uh-huh" or "uh-oh" that carried meaning but was not technically a word. One day, thinking I heard him humming a classical tune, a definite infraction of the "don't mumble" rule, I said casually, "That's nice humming," but he replied, "It's not humming. I'm saying 'do-do-do' and 'do' is a word."

His left heel still never touched the ground, and he would not write.

He would consistently avoid proximity to the "objectionable objects" and not utter the words "cigarettes" and "alcohol."

Acceptable foods were still very limited, and daytime clothing had to be bright solid colors with no brand logos. Daily hygiene procedures were usually resisted.

Winning was still essential and waiting, unreliable. Trying to hurry me one day, he yelled, "I haven't got all day!" and added, "That's what people say to me."

Above all, he needed to feel that he was in control of events and other people, and that there would be no negative consequences for anything he did. These were the deepest roots of his interaction difficulties.

Despite all these obstacles there was progress:

- Sam no longer used made-up words, could access polite words and now accepted some prompts to use them. We heard no more from the postmaster.

- His insistence on being told the time only in digital form, or to ask "How many's a couple?" seemed to fade away from lack of necessity.

- He had watched a dozen or so video movies and, with lots of negotiation, regularly accepted haircuts from me while he rewatched a familiar movie.

- We could go to the mall, grocery stores, and movies in theaters. Going to that first movie involved a long process of finding a movie we could watch ahead of time on video, theater drive-bys, lobby visits, and a generous theater manager who provided a private morning showing with a promise of no popcorn in the lobby. Two weeks later we went to a regular showing of a movie he had not already seen.

- He would eat at my house, sometimes with my family, and in a few restaurants, and he talked to clerks behind counters. And he was beginning to let me say I was proud of him.

- Sam became able to have his picture taken, after totally refusing for six of his twelve years. And after weeks of refusal, he began to ride a bike with training wheels.

He gradually became able to play briefly with the two younger children who lived next door to my family. It helped if this was pre-planned, such as having Melissa come play hide and seek, have a snack, and go home, or taking them with us to walk the corn maze. When he wanted them to go, Sam might just start chasing them like a bee, and I sometimes had to tell the kids, "Thanks for coming, but Sam wants to play alone now."

He also interacted more, though often in a bossy way, with my family. He scolded Ethan for the poster of a scantily clad model on his wall, tried to referee Ryan's basketball game with friends, and wished Kelly good luck on her college tests, adding, "You still need to know the answers." He especially liked having Dan hang him upside down and fussed playfully about Dan calling him "Amuel." One day he called his parents to say he had eaten 36 pancakes (32 were made from a drip of batter) and Dan gave him a pillow to wear home under his shirt.

In a more positive interaction with the cat, Sam rode home from the island with Micah, who hated being in the car. He talked to Micah soothingly, as if to a small child, telling him how far we had left to go by converting the miles into feet and saying the remainder of the trip was so many times the length of Micah's tail. And he never complained about the nonstop meowing.

# MEET ME WHERE I AM

Sam tolerated and participated in carefully timed discussions of how changing some behaviors could improve his life or might be essential to his future happiness and safety. But when I hoped he could avoid some unneeded conflict and just go with the flow a little he said, "I do when it's flowing my way." His conversational skills and ability to narrate an experience improved greatly over these 18 months.

We practiced taking blood pressure at home, and went, with his father, to an overdue doctor appointment, where Sam's blood pressure was measured on both arms to accommodate his symmetry need. Before we went, he had announced, "If they want blood, I'll pick a scab." Sixteen months after the oral surgery trauma, we established a new dentist. Before the first dental exam, we had driven by to admire the "FLOSM" license plate on the dentist's car, visited the waiting room, had a tour, met the people, and I bribed him for each minute he stayed in the chair.

We chipped away at adding foods a little at a time, like spaghetti with carrots grated into the sauce, grapes, and lemonade, making slight variations in clothing, tolerating handling of his left heel, accepting sunscreen, bug spray, ointment for a skin scrape, and the ever-resisted daily hygiene processes. One day he surprised me by borrowing my nail clippers and trimming his finger and toenails, after years of chewing them off.

In the June that he was thirteen, Sam received an eighth-grade certificate of completion, not a diploma. There was no high school in his town so, with Sam's parents, we were exploring options at the high school in the next town. But there was no plan in place for Sam's continued education when he made his private farewell march around the outside of the K-8 school he had attended sporadically.

# Chapter 8

# The Year Between Schools

Despite our attempts to arrange a modified high school plan that would be acceptable to Sam and to the school, we had no agreement in place when he turned fourteen that September. So, we proceeded with informal home schooling. This meant that Sam was independently learning anything academic that interested him, his parents were supporting him with resources, and I was developing potential goals related to communication, interaction and home and community life. As usual, Sam either approved, edited, or flatly rejected the goals I suggested. I continued to remove the rejected goals and describe them as future possibilities.

As it happened, we had a whole year and a second summer before Sam entered high school, so our time together focused on community activities, social interactions, life skills and a lot of related discussions and explanations.

**Community activities**: We increased the frequency and variety of our "excursions" and Sam maintained his automatic "NO!" to most of the outings I suggested. Nevertheless, during those two summers we did make many more visits to the island docks, shops, library and people's homes, and more friends visited us. Sam especially liked being on the island. Its separation from many of the mainland's noises and expectations may have helped. He often sighed contentedly, "This is a nice house/place/island." He was freer on the roads, with the people, in the places.

He ate, at last, in the restaurant on the dock, ordering a lobster roll but saying, "Hold the mayo, hold the roll." Sam was pleased when Cynthia, the owner, delivered the insides of a whole lobster, neatly arranged in its original shape, and fries with his required full bottle of ketchup. He slept alone one night in the backyard screenhouse, and I set an alarm to check on him every two hours.

After island days when we had completed several outings, Sam still needed a lengthy indoor respite of Together Time, alone activities, "no stressfuls," and sensory breaks. I included a playful "grab the (untouchable) left heel" game, which he protested but seemed to enjoy. Eventually he even initiated it.

Off the island, he finally got out of the car at the bird sanctuary, we went to the state fair and the circus, to a small indoor amusement park, miniature golf, children's museum, a small zoo, the grocery store, and a few movies and restaurants. My friend Pat sometimes came with us so Sam could have a known person sitting on each side of him. We swam at the YMCA, he got his hair cut at my salon instead of by me, and we called and rode in a smoke-free taxi. Sam practiced some independence by waiting at store entrances or on the dock while I parked the car, which he liked because it meant less walking. This generally went well until the day the mailboat was crowded, Sam panicked and created a ruckus, and the captain instructed me not to leave him alone again.

Always, our outings required advance planning, usually a visit or two to "just look" at new places from the car, and a lot of description of what to expect. Even then, I often had to say, "Okay, I'm disappointed that we can't go, but maybe another time." Sometimes, he then explained it was a control issue and now he could go. And because he still delayed departures by insisting that I put his socks and shoes on him, I continued to rub his left heel to help "heal the heel." Of course, I had to rub the right heel too.

One of our most exciting excursions came after we stopped on the way to the island to look at a coastal sightseeing plane and this boy who had previously refused to even say the names of places that couldn't be reached by land travel said he "might" like to try it "sometime." He was, of course, now traveling by boat, we had sat in a passenger plane at the airport, and we had many times pretended to send a toy man, Professor Nombre, in imaginary planes to math conferences in cities around the world. I can't count the number of times I had to recite the flight attendant's safety announcements at the beginning of all the professor's flights. When he asked for credit toward the real-life coastal plane ride as a reward for taking showers, I thought, "We might actually do this."

We planned the ten-minute sightseeing plane ride for the day I was taking him home from his island visit. Sam was quiet, less resistant to leaving the island than usual, but not showing any excitement. There were off-island delays because my sons had left the lights on in my car and the battery was dead, and a considerable wait for our turn at the airfield, but he never wavered in his decision to fly. He posed for a picture by the tiny plane, buckled in with his lips clamped shut like he was at the dentist, and held my hand tightly, but he did respond to the pilot's questions and did not complain about the very noisy, bumpy ride. Afterwards, he said he liked that the ground looked like his miniature village of Stesselville, and in a rare burst of happy excitement exclaimed, "We were up there!"

**Social interactions**: Sam's social circle was limited to mainly his family and mine and our occasionally visiting relatives and friends. He often avoided even them, and he expressed no interest in expanding this circle. He had once told his school team, "I have no use for social skills."

He would sometimes eat meals with my family, occasionally even when we had familiar guests, but often he insisted on eating alone. Sometimes he sat at a small table in the doorway between the family room and the kitchen. Once when our friends Pat and Wayne visited, I was surprised that Sam took Pat off to my office to show her something and chatted with her there for an hour. When he didn't recognize her on a later visit, I reminded him of the earlier conversation, and he again had a lengthy private chat with her. Sam often didn't recognize people he had met several times or many times, especially if they were not in their usual place or had new hairstyles.

Fooling around with Dan, our sons, or neighbor children, Sam often yelled and acted mad, even though he actually seemed to be happy and excited. His routine affect was generally neutral or annoyed. Bursts of pure happiness were rare and delightful.

After some prodding from me, Sam decided he would try to interact with "single digit" aged children. Very averse to losing, but apparently convinced that he could win, he agreed to race across an island lawn with Cole, age four, and Emma, two. As he ran, Sam loudly exhorted his legs to go faster and he did win, barely. Visiting later at their house, he wanted to play with their toys but not with them and of course, the more he complained about their presence the more they wanted to be there. He squealed at Cole for touching him, which Cole thought was a good game to repeat, and the children seemed quite fascinated by Sam and his exaggerated fussing. After she retrieved his jacket, even two-year-old Emma remarked with surprise, "He said, 'Thank you!'"

**Life skills**: We kept chipping away at the ongoing issues of hygiene, eating more varied foods, cooking, carrying his own belongings and letting go of compulsions. Hygiene continued to be difficult, but Sam's independence in travel, simple food preparation and interaction with less familiar people all seemed to progress faster at the island. And Sam's initial tiny dose of Luvox had been gradually increasing.

Sam sometimes wanted to ride short island distances alone on his bike, even going out in a light mist without complaint, but he temporarily refused to ride it at all after I mentioned possibly raising the training wheels. Because I had said training wheels were supposed to be temporary, Sam renamed them "safety wheels" or "balance wheels" and said they should be permanent.

Shortly before he turned fourteen, Sam, previously unable to admit that he dreams, asked me the meaning of a dream that he got over his left heel and symmetry issues. I said it probably meant his brain was working on it and maybe it would get better. We continued our "heal the heel" games.

A few months later, on Halloween, Sam greeted my 150 trick or treaters, as he often did, and told me that he thought two compulsions were about to go. He requested "heal the heel" games several times that day. Five days later, I asked when he thought he might be able to walk on it. Sam replied that maybe he could a little, and he put his left heel on the floor for the first time in seven years. We took photos, and he told his mother, "Don't make a big fuss." She complied. It has never been a problem since.

With no particular fanfare, Sam's need to say "Don't mumble" also faded away, but despite the dream premonition, his need for symmetrical touch remained.

**Discussions and Explanations**: Sam and I talked about lots of ordinary things, like his current interests, jokes and cartoons, news, goals and progress, videos we were watching, and places we might go. But we also invested a lot of time dealing with issues, often crises, like squirting the lady next door with the garden hose because she was smoking. He was trying to put out her cigarette.

One night, after much ado about ice cream and showers, I tried to discuss the consequences of our actions in life by demonstrating with a pencil that if you pick up one end of the stick you pick up the other end also. Not surprisingly, he "solved" the problem by breaking the pencil in half, so the consequence end stayed on the floor. But, after more conversation about reputation and damaged relationships, he did agree to help me work on the deck for a half hour to make up for a previously broken deal. Sam always wanted to reset important dented relationships to neutral, but he couldn't often accept responsibility for his share of the conflict.

Many discussions were about getting along peacefully with my family or his parents, others were about surviving in the world, our hopes for his future, explaining other people's behavior, making his point without being seen as rude, or following through on negotiated deals. We made agreements like counting silently to 300 before complaining when I stopped to talk with someone, earning rewards for toothbrushing and hair washing, and coming a bit closer than last time to places he feared.

Because people at school had tried to trick him into complying, which was outstandingly unsuccessful, Sam felt that trying to get him to change his perspective was a form of deception. And always, there was the question of who was in control. One day, while he was sitting in the apple tree reading, I brought him a shirt treated with bug spray. Sam greeted it with "NO!" I said I was just trying to spare him the pain of bug bites and he asked if I would try to force him to wear it. "No," I replied. "It's an offer. Something I'm doing for you." He took the shirt and put it on.

After a movie we enjoyed together, I commented that "We should see…" but Sam interpreted it as a demand. I explained that I just meant it would be fun to see this other movie, but he preferred different wording, saying, "I've been 'shoulded' too much!"

**School and Testing:** We did no academic work during this hiatus, but Sam did not stop learning. His mother, Beverly, bought him any book he wanted and many others she thought would interest him. They were mostly nonfiction. And he researched topics of interest on the computer.

Shortly after he turned fourteen, Sam took the Preliminary Scholastic Aptitude Test (PSAT) at the high school we had hoped he would be attending. Although the test is designed for high school juniors two to three years older than him, he scored at the 93rd percentile. But on language-based tests of social problem solving, he scored way below expectations for his age.

We never did settle on an individualized education plan at the high school most students from his town attended. So, during the second summer after eighth grade, I approached another school system where I often consulted. They were willing to allow him to try testing through some classes, after school, with hopes of gradually increasing inclusion. It was all Sam could agree to at the time.

# Chapter 9

# A Glance Back

And how does Sam now reflect on some of the events of the past few chapters?

**Authority:**

Clearly, his strong resistance to being told what to do, or not do, was a major source of conflict between Sam and everyone in his life. He says he felt as if people were trying to break him, and because he feared loss of autonomy, he became very stubborn. He now says that rules which were "on paper," were "clear and reasonable," and were "applied equally" were "more acceptable." But very few of the behaviors expected at home or school seemed to meet his criteria for acceptability.

His personal support for rules included trying to enforce elementary school ordinances that he considered essential, and later the high school dress code. Sam felt he needed to confront even minor infractions of rules because teachers were often ignoring them. These attempted enforcements did not endear him to the other students.

And how did Sam, who abhorred the idea of being punished, feel about consequences for other students who broke these rules? He says he would have been satisfied just to hear the teacher say, "Don't do that."

I asked why he had felt the need to test me by refusing simple requests and directives.

Sam: To see if you were going to try to control my environment.

Betsey: And if I passed a test?

Sam: Then you were less of a threat to my homeostasis.

Betsey: So, it was about building trust.

Sam: That is it precisely!

**Reinforcement:**

Originally, Sam saw reinforcers, rewards, or bribes as a form of control and would have no part of them. He was especially adamant that food was "a right" and even treats should never be negotiable. But after completing simple deals to earn Together Time, he began to accept some other rewards as well. Eventually, the prospect of earning a reward even allowed Sam to accept a plan he would otherwise refuse, and he would sometimes ask for one, saying, "Can I have a reward, so I won't feel forced?"

He now says that offering rewards above what a child would normally anticipate are good, but that adults expecting a child to earn something he had previously received without required effort is like "laundering a penalty."

**Medication:**

Remembering Sam's struggle to try taking a psychiatric medication or even using pain killers, ointments, and bug spray, I asked what he had been thinking about the psychiatric prescriptions. He said his initial response was, "This is one of the things I don't do." He added that he didn't want to mess around with his brain and that he heard alarm bells saying, "Bad idea; don't do it." But now, he feels that the medication has helped.

**Forgiving an affront:**

Sam has a very long memory for offenses and insists that he can't forgive an unrepented injustice. Although he now lives peacefully in an apartment attached to his parents' home, he said he doesn't believe they see him as an equal. And he is still offended that they had sometimes tried to trick or force him to do things when he was a child. Sam cited his parents' practice of keeping the candy supply in the one room where his mother smoked as evidence that they used his phobias to control him. They knew he would never enter that smokey room.

And he still believes that I should have helped him avoid oral surgery when he was twelve, saying he felt betrayed because I didn't try harder to get his approval.

He has similar strong memories of school incidents related to his behavior or his occasional peer interactions, which generally went awry. The problem is not that these home and school events occurred, but that the other participants "did not repent" for making him uncomfortable. He says now, "If I forgive something that happened ten years ago, then next time they'll say, 'He'll get over it eventually.' If it hurts now, it's important."

# MEET ME WHERE I AM

**The island:**

I asked if he knew why excursions and kitchen activities seemed easier for him on the island. Sam said his previous emotional baggage was at a greater distance in this different place, and the slower pace and smaller population made the island seem more congenial. He added that "water and greenery are said to have a salutary effect on mental health."

**My thoughts on the same topics:**

Sam had made it clear that expecting compliance was not going to be an effective way of interacting with him. So, I aimed for cooperation instead of compliance and tried to avoid any whiff of force, insistence, or demand.

To minimize his anxiety and his corresponding need to refuse or take control, I focused on:

- saying, "I'll help" rather than "You must," especially in situations where he had no choice.

- supporting exposure to new experiences, with multiple discussions before excursions about what to expect, how I would help, and why he might like it or benefit from it; guaranteeing that I would protect him at all costs and would leave with him if it became too stressful.

- collaborating on writing goals which addressed skills and behaviors we both agreed would be valuable and achievable and setting aside those he was not yet ready to attempt

- making time for relaxation, sensory breaks, and familiar Together Time play

- providing predictable earned rewards; Sam had told me at age eleven, "To a person with autism, a pleasant surprise is an oxymoron," but he did enjoy unexpected bonus rewards with specific explanation of how he earned them.

- encouraging casual and pre-arranged interactions with others-- his family and mine, friends and neighbors, church acquaintances

- maintaining my close relationship with Sam's parents and a cordial professional connection to school personnel

- setting some limits like "I won't try to make people move, but I will walk between you and them," or "First this, then that," when I knew I could make it happen; saying "I need time to think about that," instead of impulsively granting or denying his requests

- forgiving each other, and officially resetting relationships after conflicts; starting fresh and not dredging up old disagreements during new conflicts

- using personal reference books, charts, and written contracts to track progress, remember goals and verify agreements.

- supporting the gradually increasing dose of Luvox, which he still takes today.

And as for the need to accept his current reality and meet him where he is, Sam, paraphrasing the late British satirist, Terry Pratchett, says this:

**Last word**: "If you tell a psychologist that you are afraid of the monsters under your bed, the psychologist will explain that you don't need to be afraid because monsters are not real. If you say the same thing to a headologist, he will give you a fireplace poker."

# Chapter 10
# High School and Beyond

Finally, as he was turning fifteen, Sam started his highly modified high school program. I hoped this new school would be an opportunity for him to earn credits toward a diploma and be a laboratory for learning to tolerate life among more people. The IEPs we developed together still included goals for academic progress, improved interactions at home, school and the community, and ordinary life skills. And we started thinking about transition out of high school even as we transitioned in.

High school began with after school visits to meet with Algebra 1 and physical science teachers, take tests and do labs. No writing was involved, and Sam dictated math homework to his father or me, expressing some annoyance that I often mixed up the *greater than* and *less than* symbols. In October, we began to attend a few classes together, and by late November Sam was independently writing his algebra homework and tests or doing them on the computer with math symbol software his father had installed. Remarkably, despite a longtime phobia of hot or sharp objects and stainless-steel sinks, Sam began to use burners, sharp instruments and even a dirty lab sink while doing his after-school science labs.

The noise and activity of a typical high school were very stressful for Sam, but he really wanted to be there. Being there meant that when classes were changing, I often had to lead him through the halls with his eyes closed and fend off asymmetrical bumps from other students. Once, as we were leaving algebra class, and I thought he was right behind me, Sam crawled across the heating units under the windows to avoid bumping his still-seated classmates or their bookbags. We often arrived and left classes early or late to minimize the hallway trauma.

The physical education requirement was another challenge. Sam was notoriously avoidant of bodily exertion, plus the classes were noisy, action-packed, and held in an echoing gym.

## MEET ME WHERE I AM

We tried to attend a few classes in the gym, but Phys. Ed. was a non-starter. So, in February of his first year, we arranged a pass-fail course accommodation in which Sam would earn his two required years of physical education by keeping a log of 192 hours of physical exercise. We spent a lot of time in the YMCA swimming pool, took short neighborhood and woods walks, and he earned credits for time bouncing on an exercise ball, pumping a swing (finally), shelving library books, and pacing around a water-play sprinkler for half an hour. I joked that perhaps he should get PE credit for vigorously raising his hand for every question in Civics class. It took all six years, including summers, but Sam did complete his physical education requirement.

We went to a Special Olympics swim meet once when he was sixteen, but Sam refused to participate because they had misspelled his last name in the program. There was a secondary bonus though. After he watched the happy pride of both the winning and non-winning swimmers, we went back to my house and played games with none of his usual win-lose concern.

With support from school administrators and teachers who were willing to make accommodations and tolerate surprises,

Sam's high school involvement was, according to his parents, the best educational experience he had encountered.

He started ninth-grade English during the summer after his first year of high school and finished it with a different teacher during his second year. I helped more with English than with any other subject and I would have been fairly useless for the math or the more advanced science topics anyway. Sam was an avid reader, but mainly of non-fiction, so we had lots of discussions about Romeo, Juliet, Tom Sawyer, and other classic or modern characters of fiction. We invested a lot of time discussing and summarizing literature, movies, and comic strips. Sam's written responses for English class were usually dictated to me, I typed them out in a very rough draft form, and he edited them for grammar, syntax, and punctuation. We never completed an English course in one year and the British author project for Senior English was a two-year process. Sam's title was "George Orwell's *Animal Farm*: Allegory of the Soviet Union and the Threat of Totalitarian Regimes." He first dictated to me his prior knowledge of how the characters and events in Orwell's book, *Animal Farm*, represented actual history during and after the Russian Revolution of 1917. Then we went to the library so he could gather the sources to support the many facts he already knew.

---

A neuropsychological re-evaluation when Sam was eighteen resulted in confirmation of his autism, OCD and anxiety diagnoses and the addition of a diagnosis in written expression learning disability. Despite having a full-scale IQ in the very superior range, Sam showed profound difficulty with the executive functions responsible for goal-directed problem-solving behavior. He had significant difficulty inhibiting impulsive responses, very low tolerance for stress and frustration, and adaptive skills lagging ten years behind his age. The testing also indicated poor recognition and memory of people's faces and variable motor skills that may have contributed to his aversion to handwriting and athletics.

Over the six years that Sam and I went to high school once a week, he completed the required 20 credit curriculum, passed Advanced Placement physics and calculus, and earned an extra credit in statistics. His grades were mostly As and a few Bs. He earned two perfect 800s and one 750 on Scholastic Aptitude Tests.

In preparation for adult life, he completed a variety of career interest and aptitude tests, which indicated interest in science, computers, robotics, library work and proofreading. On self-assessments, Sam rated his skills high in math and science and low in understanding other people. He volunteered some in the school and public libraries and edited the church bulletins. We met with adult service providers and his parents applied for Sam's disability benefits. A trial work setting with a vocational rehabilitation worker was quickly abandoned because of his anxious, demanding behavior, which included not being able to walk into a potential work site through a front door that was flanked by a cigarette receptacle.

During those high school years, we slogged through lots of homework, and continued to practice cooking, community involvement, hygiene, shopping, medical/dental appointments, and social interactions. At school, I tried to encourage more in-class independence, saying he didn't look as grown-up with me tagging along. Sam replied with surprise, "Oh, I thought it made me look more important!"

# MEET ME WHERE I AM

**Interactions:**

As always, we spent hours discussing and negotiating ways to get along with people. Early in his first year of high school, we agreed on a list of Dos and Don'ts that we kept in a reference book with other agreements and revised every year. There were around fifteen entries including:

DO tell Betsey quietly, or sign *Go*, if you want to leave the class.

DO save teaching suggestions, classroom policy ideas, recommendations for change to discuss after class.

DON'T leave your seat to do things around the room.

DON'T direct other students' behaviors.

Despite my attempts to be clear and direct, there was room for misinterpretation, even when Sam was trying to follow through on agreements. We had agreed that he would whisper to me his comments about other people we encountered in public rather than saying them out loud. So, as I was conversing with a plump acquaintance one day, Sam did whisper, too loudly, "She's certainly a well-rounded individual."

Alcohol and smoking were still anathemas to Sam, and he would invoke the school dress code if a boy's T-shirt pocket displayed a tiny Absolut vodka bottle. He also reported seeing cleavage or extra short skirts. My suggestion that others might think he was noticing because he was interested helped curb his impulse to report these infractions of the dress code.

After years of discussions and offers of rewards, Sam became more willing to respond to greetings, but doing so in a busy high school hallway was very challenging. Even when he started keeping his eyes open in the halls, he was hyper-focused on getting where he was going without being bumped, which left little mental space for recognizing people and responding to their greetings. With his documented disability in facial recognition, he certainly couldn't identify people quickly enough to initiate a greeting, nor was he motivated to do so. I tried to alert him when one of his teachers was coming and I encouraged him to just respond, "Hi!" without trying to include the person's name if he was greeted by other students. He tried, but the greeter had usually progressed several steps beyond him before Sam spoke.

In less dynamic settings there was the additional problem of what to do about "How are you?" which he encountered several times a day. Sam's opinions on this ubiquitous social question ranged across "Why do they need to know?" "They don't really want to know," and "I can't answer because I don't know how I am." Mostly, he responded with a stony silence, and sometimes a glare, which precluded further conversation. We decided on an experiment in which he would say, "Thank you, and you?" and see if people noticed he had not really answered. He enjoyed the small deception, more conversations were able to proceed, and remarkably few people said, "Wait, you didn't answer."

Conversations with adults were always easier than those with classmates, and Sam did participate enthusiastically in class discussions. But casual interactions with other students usually had to be pre-planned, prompted and rewarded. Even then, they were infrequent.

After observing the high school graduation the year before he turned twenty, Sam opted for a private celebration at my house with family, friends, and a favorite teacher when it was his turn to graduate.

**College and living arrangement:**

After a summer of recovery, Sam began college with a Latin class taught by a friend of his social worker. He met the professor before classes began, she accommodated his handwriting difficulty, and I attended the first few classes with him. A classmate, observing Sam's comments and activity on the first day, asked me if he had autism. Sam was soon attending classes alone, driven to the university by his mother, father, or me. It helped that Stes was also on campus working as an oceanography researcher.

Sam became a familiar fixture in the university language department, where he earned mostly A grades in three semesters each of Latin, German, and Arabic, two of Spanish and Classical Greek and one each of French, Russian, Chinese, and Linguistics. The only course he took outside of the Language department was a semester on the philosophy of religion, but he did earn college credit in chemistry and biology by passing College-Level Examination Program (CLEP) exams.

He was generally tolerant of, and tolerated by, other students and faculty, but there were occasional incidents like the day he yelled at a group of students for smoking on the no-smoking campus. The students responded with a familiar hand gesture of contempt and Sam insisted on discussing the smoking policy enforcement with the campus police.

Sam stopped taking university courses after Stes retired, but he is always engaged in independent learning. Currently, he browses many topics of interest in books and on the internet which he says sometimes leads him "down a Wikipedia rabbit hole." I once told him that his six-word biography should be "Learning keeps me up at night."

# Chapter 11

# Now and Later

Over about a dozen years, Sam, his parents, and I resolved a lot of issues around survival among other people, unique communication differences, and acquiring an education. But not every compulsion that complicates his life is entirely eradicated. What remains?

**Some lingering issues:**

Sam still won't utter the words *cigarettes* or *alcohol* or any of their brand names. He now references cigarettes as " the rod of the fire of destruction" or some similar description that does not actually include saying *cigarette* or a brand name. After visiting me in my new Massachusetts home, he said he was glad I didn't live in the neighboring city. It's name was Marlborough. As for alcohol, he likes the Jeopardy term, "potent potables."

He reports that symmetrical touch is no longer a life threatening emergency but describes it as "still a strong preference." He seldom responds to "How are you?" and prefers to be called Samuel when meeting new people.

Kitchen sinks and garbage continue to be "icky" but he manages them with gloves, zip ties, an OT grabber tool, and not letting garbage get into the sink. He would love to have a cleaning person for his bathroom and kitchen every other week and says he would pay well.

Lots of downtime at home is still essential for Sam. He relaxes by sleeping, thinking, and browsing on the computer. How much downtime he requires depends on the stress level of the previous few days' events, but often he is comfortable driving to several small, nearby errands in the same day. Beverly says that before marrying Stes she could only tolerate about one event outside of home in a month.

Sam leans toward low-fashion clothing that is comfortable and easy to wear like drawstring top pants and shoes that close with Velcro. Major criteria for acceptability are that the clothing is not scratchy and he is not "a walking billboard." Sam has always refused clothing with visible brand names. I once bought him a tee shirt with his high school name and witch mascot on the pocket. The color was an acceptable bright orange but he cut out the offending pocket, leaving a large hole in the shirt.

He says that winning a game is now not an issue per se, but he is stressed if his parents claim that a Scrabble rule is official when he believes it is their adaptation. He says that even if he understands and agrees with the reason for the rule, he can't accept that they don't admit it was their decision.

But, Sam lives in his own apartment, drives a car and goes to the grocery store, farmers' market, and YMCA swimming pool, both with his father and alone. Recently, he drove himself alone to the dentist, had an unplanned root canal and drove home.

He cooks meat and fish in the oven, bread in a bread machine, and he now eats peas, broccoli, potatoes and carrots "in some contexts." He eats dinner with his parents more nights than not, and Bev says he cleared his couch and lift-top coffee table so he could have them to dinner in his apartment. She reports that he shares the food he purchases at the farmers' market, helps carry in heavy items like flats of water bottles and bags of stove pellets and is making more housekeeping efforts in his apartment attached to their house. His parents hope Sam may someday live in his apartment with renters in the main house. They continue working on financial and support resources for the years he will survive them.

Sam has enjoyed conversation and some community excursions with two different adult support workers. Unfortunately, both men have resigned to attend to other responsibilities in their lives. Bev is hoping Sam's adult services agency will be able to find another compatible worker for Sam. He would like this too, but feels it is not urgent and that his social life, which involves mainly contact with his parents and their visitors, is okay as it is. "Other people," says Sam, "are best appreciated in small quantities."

**Quality of life**

The quality of one's life refers to the degree to which an individual is healthy, comfortable, and able to participate in or enjoy life events. It's an ambiguous and subjective term, as *quality of life* can refer both to the ways individuals view their own lives and to their living conditions.

I asked Sam recently what he needed for a good quality of life and he responded, "My own living area with reliable power all the time, food I can eat, and comfortable temperatures I can control myself. I need control over my choices; I'm the only one who knows exactly what I need." He said that he required enough money to support his quality of life needs and added, "If I had millions of dollars it would go toward supporting other people's quality of life."

**Future hopes and needs**

Sam would like to "solidify his quality of life, to have his own family, and to go places." He mentioned wanting to visit the Smithsonian, Mount Rushmore, and "the great landscapes of our country." He would also like to see a space launch.

We discussed the possibility of employment and his needs if he did work. I assumed he would want part time and remote employment, but he said that would depend on the job. Sam couldn't readily name work he would enjoy, but among some possibilities I mentioned he endorsed proofreading, editing, teaching or tutoring, political research, or working with maps. We agreed that he would not want manual labor, a busy work site or outdoor employment. Asked if he would he be willing to get more credentials if needed, Sam replied, "Yes, that wouldn't be difficult." How would he feel about working in a team with others? Sam acknowledged that he does often prefer working by himself but would like to work with "other people like me who don't engage in chit-chat and meaningless conversation" if they were tolerant of non-conformists. As for work supports, Sam would look for flexibility, being able to ask for accommodations, and having instructions provided in writing.

**Trauma-Informed Support?**

Both autism and OCD are associated with considerable anxiety, and anxiety often provokes a powerful need for control. All were rampant in Sam. He says, "With OCD things got stuck. I couldn't be accommodating even if I wanted to."

I told Sam that autistic adults have described childhood and adult life with autism as a form of trauma, because of the ongoing stress of living in a confusing neurotypical world, struggling with interactions at school and work, and often feeling that the intensity of their struggles was invalidated by other people. He replied, "I think that's a fair description." He thought that in our work together we had done, "fairly well" in applying the suggested trauma-informed supports of safety, trustworthiness, choice, collaboration and empowerment although we had never heard the term, *trauma-informed support*. After all, Sam said, "A lot of things get developed independently, like Newton and Leibniz separately and independently developing calculus."

---

Given that autism and OCD present challenges that leave people out of sync with the neurotypical world, anxiety is almost inevitable. In many cases, that anxiety leads to resistant behavior, and sometimes to an extreme need to avoid the expectations of others and to impose significant control over one's environment. As Sam and I would attest, it is very difficult to navigate the world comfortably with autism or OCD, and combining the two diagnoses multiplies the complications. A high IQ does not equate with a low need for support, and for some students the accommodations and expectations in an IEP need to be very individualized indeed.

"Meet me where I am" does not mean "just accommodate around my difficulties." It is simply a starting point chosen to make progress more possible. For Sam and I, this meant accepting his personal realities, like the postmaster and many compulsions, and accommodating his immediate needs, while encouraging and assisting him to adapt to more of the world's expectations. It also meant minimizing unwinnable confrontations and incentivizing collaboration and cooperation.

With considerable individualizing of his IEP, Sam completed a public school education and many college courses. He lives semi-independently and is comfortable with the quality of his life. Is he done? No one alive is ever done. Child development becomes adult development; more skills lead to more competence and confidence, creating less anxiety and wider opportunities. I wish for Sam an adult life of self-chosen experiences that will continue to build his happiness and independence.

**Our last word**

We all travel through life on different roads with different-sized obstacles and goals, but the trip is easier when people meet us where we are and we guide each other around the rough spots.

# Acknowledgments

I especially want to thank Samuel P. Stessel who lived this story with me and willingly shared and reflected on it for our readers. We both learned and grew from our time together.

Special thanks to Sam's mother, Beverly Stessel, for designing the wonderfully meaningful cover for <u>Meet Me Where I Am: Navigating the Intersection of Autism and OCD.</u> Her cover illustrates how the trees along the rocky road of autism and those by the tight brick structure of "OCD Street" converge to create a canopy over the path of a whole life.

I truly appreciate the hours of listening and advising given freely by the members of the Hudson Public Library Writers Group and our leader, Tiana Gorham, as I wrote this book.

And thanks to Samuel and his parents, who read and repaired the whole manuscript and to Gail Tudor, Judy Meyers, and Emma Green, who each read and commented on several chapters.

**Works Cited**

"Granny Weatherwax." *Wikipedia, The Free Encyclopedia,* Wikimedia Foundation, 14 January 2023,https://en.m.wikipedia.org/wiki/Granny_Weatherwax#:~:text=It%20has%20been%20said%20that,a%20chair%20to%20stand%20on

Markham, Edwin. *The Shoes of Happiness and Other Poems.* The Century Company, 1913.

"Susan Sto Helit" *Wikipedia, The Free Encyclopedia,* Wikimedia Foundation,

https://en.wikipedia.org/wiki/Susan_Sto_Helit accessed April 3rd, 2023,

at 2:28 pm EDT 6:28 UTC

# About Author

In addition to this book, a work of narrative nonfiction about the intersection of autism and OCD, Elizabeth Ives Field is the author of <u>Building Communication and Independence for Children Across the Autism Spectrum: Strategies to Address Minimal Language, Echolalia and Behavior</u> (2021) London, Jessica Kingsley Publishers.

Elizabeth, also known as Betsey, has provided speech/language therapy and communication/behavior consultation to autism families and educators for over 45 years and has presented at national and regional conferences on topics of autism and communication. She has particular interest in, and considerable experience with, echolalia and autism in both sighted and blind/visually impaired children.

## ELIZABETH IVES FIELD

She now lives in Hudson, Massachusetts, does webinars and conference presentations, and writes books and articles on autism topics. Find her on LinkedIn at http://www.linkedin.com/in/elizabeth-ives-field